Let's learn to think creatively

9 BEST IDEAS FOR LEARNING TO THINK CREATIVELY

by

Pro Ahmad

Contents

Introduction *8*
1. Identify your ability and field *11*

Meaning of finding yourself? 11

Some exercises to find yourself: 13

Some haibits to find yourself: 15
2. Observing a new path everyday. *19*

Introduction 19

Exploration's Potential 19

Physical Routes 20

Mental Routes 21

Paths of Daily Routine 22

The Social Advantages of Exploring New Ideas 22

Great Communication 23

Developing Empathy 24

Dismantling obstacles 24

Promoting Cooperation 24

Motivating Others 25

Improving Problem-Solving 25

Creating a Network of Support 26

Conclusion 27
3- Be frank and expand relationships *28*

Let's learn to think creatively   3

1. Frankness for creative thinking: 28

2. Expanding relationship for creative thinking:................ 32

Relationships and Creativity: A Connection 33

Relationships with others and original thought................. 34

Relationships and artistic exploration 34

The Creative Spark in Romantic Relationships 35

Mentoring and Creative Development................................. 35

Collaboration with colleagues and innovation................... 35

Culture at Work and Creative Freedom 36

Teams working together across disciplines 36

connecting people and innovative entrepreneurship........ 36

Taking Charge and Supporting Creative Teams................ 37

Relationships Increasing in the Digital Age........................ 37

Technology's Impact on Relationships and Creativity 37

Social media, chance, and motivation.................................. 38

Exploring creative niches and online communities........... 38

The Study of Increasing Relationships for Creative
     Thinking.. 38

Science of the Brain and the Creative Mind 39

Case Studies and research 39

Overcoming Obstacles to Developing New Relationships39

Relationship building, shyness, and introversion.............. 40

The Science of Juggling Relationships 40

Global Creativity and Cultural Diversity............................ 40

The Importance of Cultural Exchange for Creativity 40

Creative diplomatic relations and diplomacy 41

The Evolution of Relationships and Creativity in the
    Future 41

Innovations in Technology and Creative Possibilities 41

Creating a Culture of Connection through Creativity 42

Conclusion 42
6. Prepare your mind for any occasion 43

Introduction 43

The Practice of Creativity... 43

Knowing the Mind's Function in Creativity 44

Getting the Mind Ready for Original Thought.................. 44

Knowledge of the Creative Process.................................... 44

I. Identifying the issue or difficulty.................................... 45

II. Information and Inspiration Gathering 45

III. Embryology 45

IV. The 'Aha' Experience: The Eureka Moment.................. 46

V. Assessment and Improvement.. 46

Techniques for Mental Preparation for Creativity 46

Let's learn to think creatively   5

1.Develop a Growth Mindset. 46

2. Look for a Variety of Experiences 47

3. Meditation and mindfulness 47

4. Make Use of the Brainstorming Power 47

5. Create a Culture of Creativity 48

6. Accept Diverse Points of View 48

7. Exercises for Creative Thinking 48

8. Ongoing Education and Skill Building 48

Mentally Getting Ready for Different Situations 49

1. Originality of self 49

2. Expertise in Creativity 49

3. Innovative Issue-Solving 49

4. Innovation and the Creative Arts 50

Conclusion 50
7. Be curious and develop a passion for learning 51

Introduction 51

I. The Pith of Interest 51

II. The Part of Deep rooted Learning 52

III. How Interest and Long lasting Learning Improve
       Inventive Considering 53

IV. Developing Interest and Deep rooted Learning 54

V. How Interest and Long lasting Learning Influence

Diverse Viewpoints of Life.. 54

Summary 59
8- Trusting your mind and not waiting for
inspiration 60

A Brief Introduction... 60

I. The Myths of Imaginative Motivation............................ 60

II. The Inventive Intellect: A Wellspring of Advancement61

III. Overcoming Creative Blocks.................................... 62

IV. The Part of Mentality in Imaginative Considering 62

V. Trusting Your Intellect totally Different Perspectives of
Life 63

VI. The Inventive Prepare: A Guided Travel..................... 64

VII. The Affect of Trusting Your Intellect on Society 64

VIII. Supporting Your Imaginative Intellect within the
Computerized Age 65

IX. Challenges in Trusting Your Intellect 66

Conclusion 66
9- Learn to ignore problems... 68

Introduction 68

I. The Myth of Never-ending Problem-Solving................... 68

II. Grasping Cognitive Opportunity 69

III. Disparate Considering and Inventiveness 69

IV. Getting away Mental Traps.. 70

V. Creativity and the Control of Play 70

VI. Adjusting Numbness and Obligation 71

VII. Application in Individual Development 71

VIII. Cultivating a Culture of Inventiveness 72

IX. Challenges in Grasping Numbness 72

X. The Computerized Age and Data Over-burden 73

XI. Victory Stories in Inventive Obliviousness 73

Conclusion 74

INTRODUCTION

Creative thinking could be a principal angle of human cognition that plays a significant part in different viewpoints of life, from problem-solving to development and individual development. It is the capacity to produce unique and inventive thoughts, arrangements, and points of view that go past routine boundaries. This shape of considering is characterized by a eagerness to break free from built up standards, challenge the status quo, and investigate unused conceivable outcomes.

The significance of creative thinking cannot be exaggerated. It may be a driving constrain behind development, permitting people and organizations to create groundbreaking items, administrations, and forms. Inventive considering is the start that powers advance in areas such as innovation, craftsmanship, science, and commerce. Without it, we would be stuck in a interminable cycle of stagnation and missed openings for development and change.

Additionally, imaginative considering has various benefits on a individual level. It improves problem-solving aptitudes, empowering people to handle complex issues with new viewpoints and adjust to changing circumstances. It cultivates versatility and versatility, as inventive scholars are more open to alter and superior prepared to overcome impediments. Additionally, it advances self-expression, self-discovery, and self-confidence, engaging people to investigate their interesting talents and concepts.

In a progressively energetic and interconnected world, inventive considering may be a profitable resource, making a difference us explore the complexities of our ever-evolving society and motivating the arrangements required to address its challenges. This initial concept highlights the basic part imaginative considering plays in forming our future and the monstrous benefits it offers to people and society as an entire.

Among other things, these pages will help

you to:

- develop your understanding of the creative process;

- overcome barriers or blocks to having new ideas;

- enlarge your parameters of vision;

- learn to build on ideas as well as criticize them;

- increase your tolerance for uncertainty and doubt;

- listen, look and read with a creative attitude;

- make time to think;

- Become more confident in yourself as a creative person.

1. IDENTIFY YOUR ABILITY AND FIELD

Nature has created every human being different from others and it has created many features that make it different and distinguished from others so It is very foolish to say that every person can do everything and achieve success in every field

Remember that many people fail in the world because they don't know what they have in them to succeed in. While looking at others, they have been working hard in fields according to which their personality has not been created

To better your well-being and discover your purpose and passions in life, you're going to need a jumping-off point. Some direction and a better understanding of how to find yourself on the road to self-discovery will help you start.

Meaning of finding yourself?

Finding yourself occurs when you become

aware of who you are as a person and something clicks in your head. Everyone's interpretation of this will be different, but it ultimately centers on what you want from life.

You could be wondering how understanding who you are affects your life. You'll be able to embrace your sentiments and identity as well as pinpoint your objectives and driving forces if you have a clearer understanding of your basic principles and who your genuine self is.

Being the best versions of ourselves doesn't entail being perfect or constantly shining with joy. It indicates that we have improved self-esteem and mental well-being and that we resist giving in to external pressure.

This wasn't an easy assignment to complete. Your inner voice is going to speak a lot when you're searching for yourself, which can be very distracting. But through both wonderful and negative life experiences, we come to terms with who we are and aren't.

It requires you to fit the puzzle pieces together, identify the gaps in your life, and learn the necessary procedures to close those gaps. On your journey, exercises like creating a personal vision statement can be helpful.

Ultimately, finding ourselves boosts our self-confidence, self-esteem, and our self-awareness. You'll know yourself better than anyone else does.

Some exercises to find yourself:

Example No. 1: An example may be the best explanation to identify yourself, Select ten stanzas from different fields and fix your issues with them Meet them, give gifts and get close, Get close enough that they get to know you and don't feel nervous sharing anything about their lives.

When you get to know them and they get to know you, take a register and a pencil and write their names on each page.

Talk to them for half an hour daily on various topics and ask questions related to their field, Ask the secret of their growth, Ask the causes of problems in their life and how to solve these problems.

In short, feel free to mingle with them and chat for half an hour every day and come home every day and write your comments about the time spent with them and give them stars or numbers.

You should continue this exercise for a month and write down your comments about the moments you spend with them every day

Read carefully the comments you have written about each person in a month and add up the number of marks you have given them.

Of these, the one to whom you score the highest in conversation is the one to whom your temperament and nature is most inclined, for human nature is most inclined to that which it sees as a soul like itself.

Example No. 2: A friendly example of this could be to buy some books on different subjects and arts and read them carefully every day.

Now go on writing your comments about each book. After a few days, you can estimate which book you have written more and more positive comments about, as if your nature and nature is closer to the art of the art book you read. Higher marks are given

Example No. 3: A third example would be to start collecting scholarly and literary material on various subjects or arts for a month and write a short commentary on that material.

After a month, show your collected material and your comments to a thinker who will easily be able to tell you in which field you can work better.

Some haibits to find yourself:

The habits you need to figure out who you are cannot be purchased at a store. Although there isn't a step-by-step guide for discovering your true self, you can go within and create certain mindful habits that will help you when traveling.

Finding yourself is a path full of obstacles that can make us question our self-worth and cast seeds of doubt everywhere. When you're on your way to finding yourself, make it a habit to practice self-care. You can do this through positive self-talk and affirmations that you say to yourself each morning or when you write them down in a journal.

Never think negatively about anything you notice about yourself. People typically don't identify their own finest traits, preferring instead to value other people's qualities while disregarding their own. As a result, they think negatively of themselves and assume that they might not be able to think constructively and creatively.

It should be that a person should find positive and creative use of whatever qualities he sees in himself.

You might also develop the habit of being open during this procedure.

Discuss your struggles with a family member, a close friend, or a coach. Discussing it with others can help you feel at ease and provide you with plans for the future. If you're tempted to relapse into negative behaviors, hearing other people's viewpoints can serve as inspiration.

It's not easy to stick to a long-term goal. A Better Up coach can provide the accountability you need for discovering yourself without feeling overwhelmed and exhausted.

Similarly, always associate yourself with positive and high-minded people, Respect and choose the best fields and get close to the people who run them

Find and study bestselling books as well as read about their authors' lives.

Always believe in action, always stay away from empty slogans and just talk, try to learn from religion, include its book in your study and always write down its points in a notebook

The habit of studying makes one's mind very strong and capable of effective communication as well as making sound decisions

If one keeps making a list of the most important topics and points during his studies, then one's life becomes more civilized and orderly.

Learn to differentiate between people, Respect someone as much as they deserve. One thing always keep in your mind that giving more respect to a less respectable person makes him worse, and treating a more respectable person as inferior and contemptible can make him distant from you.

Always learn to share respect and kindness Always respect elders even if they are less than you in knowledge and practice

Never make them believe that they are somehow inferior to you. Always be kind to the little ones. Behave with the little ones in such a way that they aspire and want to be like you. Build dignity among your peers and own your own self and personality.

These are all great habits that you can adopt to find yourself, take stock of yourself, plan your future, choose your path to success and decide your good and bad.

2. OBSERVING A NEW PATH EVERYDAY.

Introduction

It's easy to get stuck in patterns that leave us feeling stagnant and uninspired in the midst of our daily lives. Observing a different path every day, on the other hand, is a simple yet powerful exercise that may infuse your life with newness, curiosity, and a revitalized feeling of wonder. Embracing this practice, whether it's a physical journey, a mental journey, or a new attitude to your daily routine, can lead to a more full and enriching existence.

Exploration's Potential

Taking a new path every day is about more than simply physical exploration; it's about cultivating a curious and open-minded mindset. We tap into the great power of exploration when we make a conscious effort to seek out fresh experiences and viewpoints.

Expanding Horizons: We broaden our horizons when we observe a new path, whether it's taking a different route to work, trying a new activity, or traveling to an unusual location. We break free from our habits and expose ourselves to new ideas, cultures, and ways of thinking.

Creating New Experiences: New experiences encourage our creativity. They push our minds to think differently, solve issues, and experience the world in new ways. This can result in successes in both personal and professional activities.

Building Resilience: Taking on new challenges increases resilience and flexibility. When faced with unforeseen challenges, we learn to problem solve and persevere. This resilience can help us tackle life's obstacles with more confidence and grace over time.

Physical Routes

Nature Trails: Exploring the natural world is one of the simplest methods to observe a new path. Hike into a local woodland, stroll along a riverside, or explore a park you've never seen before. Nature provides limitless options for exploration.

Urban Adventures: There are probably innumerable streets, lanes, and neighborhoods in the heart of your city or town that you've never explored. Set out on foot or by bike and you'll be delighted at the hidden treasures you'll find.

Mental Routes

Diverse Reading: Reading books and articles on a variety of topics might expose you to different ideas and perspectives. Experiment with reading something outside your regular genres or regions of interest.

Learning a New Skill: Whether it's picking up a new language, painting, or playing a musical instrument, learning a new skill takes you on a cerebral trip of growth and discovery.

Deep Conversations: Hold meaningful discussions with people from various backgrounds and worldviews. These discussions can be eye-opening and expand your worldview.

Paths of Daily Routine

Change up Your Commute: Instead of driving the same route every day, consider utilizing public transportation or biking. You'll see familiar sights from a different angle.

Culinary Exploration: Try new foods or dine at establishments serving cuisine you've never tried before. Food is a delightful way to learn about other cultures.

Mindful Living: Practice awareness by observing the current moment objectively. This might help you appreciate the beauty and amazement that surrounds you every day.

As a person sees new ways every day, new thoughts and ideas are born in his mind. He gets inspired by the environment and gets ideas for something new while visiting the roads

The Social Advantages of Exploring New Ideas

Thinking about fresh ideas is a valuable instrument not only for personal development and innovation, but also for improving our social lives. Accepting new viewpoints and thinking can have a significant impact on our interactions with others and our position in our communities. In this post, we'll look at the social benefits of considering new ideas and how they can lead to more meaningful and richer interactions.

Great Communication

Improving communication is among the most important social benefits of considering novel concepts. We improve our communication skills when we converse with people who have different viewpoints and views. We improve our ability to speak clearly, ask questions, and actively listen.

We can use this improved communication ability when interacting with friends, family, and coworkers. We can have richer, more meaningful conversations and build closer relationships with those around us when we are receptive to new ideas.

Developing Empathy

Thinking about new concepts frequently entails taking into account multiple perspectives and comprehending distinct experiences. This process encourages empathy, which is essential for positive social relationships. Since empathy helps us comprehend others' thoughts, feelings, and views better, it enables us to relate to them on a deeper level.

Dismantling obstacles

Accepting new concepts can aid in removing social and cultural obstacles. Stereotypes and biases that may make it difficult for us to connect with others are challenged when we actively seek out and engage with different points of view.

We can communicate with others from various backgrounds thanks to our open minds, which promotes a more welcoming and peaceful social setting.

Promoting Cooperation

Collaboration amongst people with different backgrounds and viewpoints is frequently the source of innovation. We foster an environment where cooperation flourishes when we actively consider fresh ideas and encourage others to do the same.

Innovative solutions are produced by collaborative efforts, which can also strengthen social ties. Accepting new ideas promotes collaboration and a sense of shared purpose, whether it be at work, in community projects, or within our social networks.

Motivating Others

Your excitement for considering novel concepts has the potential to spread. You encourage others to do the same when you actively participate in debates regarding cutting-edge ideas and show that you are receptive to new viewpoints.

By inspiring others to venture outside their comfort zones and adopt novel concepts, your openness to new ideas can serve as a catalyst for positive change in your social networks.

Improving Problem-Solving

Thinking about novel concepts improves

our ability to solve problems. Our capacity to tackle these issues with creativity and new perspectives might result in more efficient solutions when we face difficulties in our social lives, whether they include individual conflicts or communal issues.

We can solve social problems more effectively and sustain healthy relationships within our communities by embracing innovative thinking.

Creating a Network of Support

People who actively consider novel concepts frequently draw other like-minded people who share their enthusiasm for creativity and open-mindedness. This can result in the development of a strong network of friends, coworkers, and mentors who support and push one another to develop and flourish.

A network like this can offer important social support and act as a source of motivation and inspiration.

It has a significant impact on our social lives and goes beyond personal growth. By welcoming new ideas, encouraging empathy, and actively interacting with opposing points of view, we improve our communication abilities, dismantle obstacles, and motivate constructive change in our communities.

Relationships become deeper and more fulfilling as a result of thinking about new concepts, which also helps society as a whole evolve and innovate. In order to change your social connections and enrich your life, make a conscious effort to explore and share fresh ideas.

<u>Conclusion</u>

Taking a new path every day is a discipline that can give your life fresh life and significance. It inspires you to embrace the unknown, to seek adventure in both the familiar and the unfamiliar, and to grow as a person. You can create a deeper, more rewarding existence and become a lifelong explorer of the world around you by taking little steps each day to observe new paths. So, why bother? Begin today and begin your voyage of exploration!

3- BE FRANK AND EXPAND RELATIONSHIPS

1. Frankness for creative thinking:

Bluntness, frequently characterized as the quality of being open, fair, and direct in one's communication, could be a ethicalness that has been celebrated over societies and centuries. It is the establishment upon which believe, understanding, and important associations are built. In this advanced age of fast-paced communication, where realness can now and then be dominated by channels and exteriors, the significance of forthrightness cannot be emphasized sufficient.

This article investigates the multifaceted noteworthiness of forthrightness in our lives, diving deep into the social benefits it offers. We are going look at how forthrightness cultivates believe, improves connections, advances individual development, and contributes to generally well-being. By the conclusion of this comprehensive investigation, you'll not as it were get it the esteem of bluntness but moreover be propelled to develop it in your possess life.

Man is a creature who makes life good or bad on the basis of his mind. If the mind is suffering from many confusions and a person cannot get rid of them, then surely a person will not be able to enjoy the environment around him. He will not know the colors of the world, new ideas will not come to his mind, he will not be able to think about progress.

The world will become a prison for him; he will remain a collection of negative thoughts. Some sense of his own good and bad will not exist in him. There will even come a time when it will be difficult to spend time for it. Gradually he will become a house of problems, a time will come when he will be made an incurable patient and thrown into a madhouse.

Now such problems may be a part of every human's life, but the solution to all of them is that humans create a friendly environment with others. Share the problems that burden your mind with others. It is a principle of psychology that sharing reduces problems. This person should recognize friends and discuss his problems with his sincere friends. Listen to their problems and tell them your problems. Talk to them about the country's situation.

When he hears about his culture and expresses his apologetic conscience, when he starts sharing, the burden will begin to come off his mind. His negative thoughts will begin to diminish and gradually he will begin to heal himself.

Here we have to examine both directions

On the one hand, the man, the only son, was lost in negative thoughts and those things were the cause of increasing his troubles day by day, all people became alien to him.

He had forgotten the difference between the little ones and the big ones, As a result of all this, he became a mental patient and was admitted to an insane asylum

On the other hand, he created a friendly

atmosphere with the people, Listen to people's problems and tell them your problems. He shared in people's happiness and he shared his happiness with others. Due to which the burden of his mind continued to lighten, His negative thoughts kept disappearing, His mind kept turning to something new. As a result, he became an excellent citizen of the society

Now if we go to the foundation and think, we will know that the person entered the madhouse as a mental patient, this was because he did not establish a friendly environment with others

On the other hand, the person who became a respectable citizen in spite of many problems, He had established a friendly environment with others due to which his worries disappeared on a daily basis and he is leading a happy life.

As if from here we can draw the conclusion that by adapting our society in a friendly environment we can live a good life despite the problems.

And by not having a friendly environment,

we can make even a good society a hell and more trouble for ourselves.

Therefore, we should understand that due to the lack of a friendly environment, we will be mentally disturbed. There will be a collection of negative thoughts and will not be able to think anything creative.

Whereas due to friendly conversion our daily problems will be removed and we will live as good citizens. Our mind will be fresh and we will be able to possess the best creative thinking.

2. Expanding relationship for creative thinking:

Introduction

The core of creativity is human connection. The breadth and variety of our relationships have a significant impact on our capacity for original thought, problem-solving, and innovation. The profound significance of strengthening relationships for releasing creative potential is explored in this article. It explores the processes by which social interactions, in both the personal and professional spheres, foster creativity. You'll have a thorough understanding of how creating a network of interesting, meaningful connections can promote an environment that encourages creativity and innovation by the end of this investigation.

Expanding relationships are crucial for creative thinking in the constantly changing context of human existence. Our ability to think creatively is greatly influenced by the breadth and depth of our relationships, whether they be interpersonal, professional, or societal. This article examines the profound importance of fostering meaningful relationships and their profound influence on our capacity to create and be inspired.

Relationships and Creativity: A Connection

Fundamentally, creativity is a dynamic force that stimulates originality, innovation, and problem-solving. It is closely related to how we interact with others. Whether fleeting or ongoing, our interactions have the potential to have an impact on our creative processes in ways we may not always fully understand.

Relationships with others and original thought

Family Structure and Creative Process

Our ability to be creative can be greatly influenced by the relationships we have with our families when we are young. The foundation for encouraging creative thinking can be found in a loving and supportive family setting. Children are encouraged to explore their ideas in such an environment, and this encouragement frequently persists into adulthood.

Relationships and artistic exploration

Friendships, which are the foundation of personal relationships, offer us a diverse range of viewpoints and experiences. Our horizons are broadened by diverse friendships, which expose us to a range of perspectives and foster teamwork in creative endeavors. The excitement of mutual discovery and the cross-pollination of ideas are what give brainstorming with friends their special magic.

The Creative Spark in Romantic Relationships

While romantic relationships are frequently studied for their emotional components, they also play a critical role in stimulating creativity. These connections provide a special fusion of emotional support, shared inspiration, and creative pursuits that can spark original thought.

Mentoring and Creative Development

Another method for fostering new interpersonal connections that foster creativity is through mentor-mentee relationships. A mentor can offer advice, share experiences, and encourage their mentees to think creatively. Knowledge and wisdom exchange acts as a source of inspiration.

Collaboration with colleagues and innovation

Professional relationships have a transformative effect in the workplace, which serves as a crucible for innovative thinking. An environment that is favorable to innovation fosters a collaborative and unrestricted exchange of ideas culture.

Culture at Work and Creative Freedom

Creative freedom is supported in a progressive workplace environment. Employees are encouraged to challenge conventional wisdom and consider novel ideas in such a setting. Hierarchical structures that in more conventional settings may stifle creativity are destroyed.

Teams working together across disciplines

Innovation in the workplace is built on a foundation of collaboration. Cross-disciplinary teams made up of people from different backgrounds bring a diversity of viewpoints to the table, igniting creative synergies that may result in game-changing concepts.

connecting people and innovative entrepreneurship

Professional networks are troves of inventive possibilities and potential collaborators. By extending your network, you can access the combined knowledge and creative potential of a wide range of people and organizations.

Taking Charge and Supporting Creative Teams

Organizational leaders are essential in fostering and supporting creativity among their teams. A supportive, creative boss creates an environment where staff members feel free to experiment, come up with ideas, and challenge conventional wisdom.

Relationships Increasing in the Digital Age

The way we establish and maintain relationships has changed dramatically in the digital age. Technology-enabled global connectivity has created new opportunities for communication and imaginative thought.

Technology's Impact on Relationships and Creativity

The nature of relationships has changed as a result of technology. While it has presented difficulties, such as maintaining real connections in a digital environment, it has also created previously unimaginable opportunities for creative interaction.

Social media, chance, and motivation

Platforms for social media provide distinctive chances for creative serendipity. Online connections can create unanticipated opportunities for inspiration and teamwork. The world of technology has evolved into a creative and innovative hub.

Exploring creative niches and online communities

Online communities offer places where people with specialized interests can congregate to share ideas and be inspired by one another. These communities, which are frequently built around particular interests, encourage creativity by providing a welcoming environment for experimentation and innovation.

The Study of Increasing Relationships for Creative Thinking

The intricate relationships between relationship expansion and creative thinking are being illuminated by scientific research.

Science of the Brain and the Creative Mind

Researchers in neuroscience are starting to identify the neural connections between creative thinking and interpersonal relationships. Different kinds of relationships trigger different brain functions, which have an impact on our creative processes.

Case Studies and research

Studies examining the connection between relationship growth and original thought are instructive. They offer verifiable proof of the link between increasing one's social and professional networks and innovative breakthroughs.

Overcoming Obstacles to Developing New Relationships

Expanding relationships has significant advantages for creativity, but it's also important to address any difficulties that might arise.

Relationship building, shyness, and introversion

Increasing their social networks can be particularly difficult for introverts. It's imperative to develop methods for overcoming shyness and utilizing introversion's capacity for original thought.

The Science of Juggling Relationships

It's crucial to keep the delicate balance between relationships and one's own wellbeing. Exhaustion from overcommitting to relationship growth can impair one's ability to produce creatively.

Global Creativity and Cultural Diversity

Creative thinking is significantly impacted by cultural diversity. The diversity of thoughts that result from the mingling of various cultures can spark creative responses to pressing global issues.

The Importance of Cultural Exchange for Creativity

Cultural exchange provides access to new

viewpoints and insights that have the power to transform creative thinking. Innovative solutions and artistic endeavors are produced through the collaborative efforts of people from various backgrounds.

Creative diplomatic relations and diplomacy

On a global scale, diplomacy is essential for building relationships and encouraging original thinking. Political, cultural, and social barriers are crossed through diplomatic relations, fostering environments that encourage original solutions to global problems.

The Evolution of Relationships and Creativity in the Future

The potential for relationship growth to fuel creativity is limitless as we march into the future.

Innovations in Technology and Creative Possibilities

Artificial intelligence and virtual reality, two emerging technologies, are poised to redefine our interpersonal interactions and creative possibilities. The way we cooperate and innovate could be completely changed by these technologies.

Creating a Culture of Connection through Creativity

The development of a culture of creative connection in which businesses and people alike value interpersonal interaction holds promise for the future. We can foster an environment where innovation thrives through education, policy, and the development of creative communities.

Conclusion

There is no denying the link between developing relationships and original thought. It is a dynamic force that affects all aspects of our lives—personal, professional, and even international diplomacy. We can unlock the doors to creativity, innovation, and inspiration by embracing the power of relationships, which will lead us toward a future that is brighter and more connected.

6. PREPARE YOUR MIND FOR ANY OCCASION

Introduction

In a world marked by constant change and innovation, the ability to think creatively is dynamic and essential. The capacity to think creatively is a strong asset in all aspects of life, including personal and professional endeavors as well as tackling global challenges. The significance of preparing your mind for any situation is one aspect of creative thinking that is frequently overlooked. This article explores the profound value of mental preparation for fostering original thought and offers information on the methods and approaches that can be used to do so.

The Practice of Creativity

The ability to come up with original ideas, find solutions to issues, and see the world from new perspectives is creativity. It is a multifaceted skill with a wide range of applications in all facets of our lives.

Creativity is the force that advances humanity, propelling it forward in fields like the arts, sciences, and everyday problem-solving.

Knowing the Mind's Function in Creativity

The center of creativity is the mind. It is the environment in which concepts are created and raised. The mind is not a static thing, though. It can be shaped and is adaptable to its environment, its experiences, and the deliberate preparation it goes through.

Getting the Mind Ready for Original Thought

The process of getting the mind ready is not universal. It varies depending on the person and the situation. Here, we look at the various ways you can get your mind ready for creative thinking so you can approach any situation with the originality and ingenuity that creativity brings.

Knowledge of the Creative Process

Understanding the creative process itself is crucial before diving into mental planning.

Creativity is a systematic progression of ideas, frequently involving several stages, rather than a flash of genius. Understanding this procedure makes for more effective mental planning.

I. Identifying the issue or difficulty

Identification and expression of the current issue or challenge are frequently the first steps in the creative process. This stage necessitates a thorough comprehension of the problems that demand original solutions.

II. Information and Inspiration Gathering

Information is essential for creativity. A key component of mental preparation is gathering a variety of information, viewpoints, and inspiration. The components of original ideas can be found in a diverse collection of knowledge.

III. Embryology

The information must be given time to simmer in the mind during the incubation phase. In this passive stage, your subconscious mind fills in the blanks and creates new associations. During this phase, you should mentally prepare by making an environment that will allow your mind to work quietly in the background.

IV. The 'Aha' Experience: The Eureka Moment

The creative breakthrough known as the "Eureka moment" occurs when ideas that were frequently formed during the incubation phase suddenly come to the fore. The probability of having these moments increases with mental preparation.

V. Assessment and Improvement

Being creative involves not only coming up with ideas but also analyzing and improving them. The mind must be ready to receive criticism and feedback.

Techniques for Mental Preparation for Creativity

1.Develop a Growth Mindset.

A growth mindset is the conviction that

aptitude and intelligence can be improved with commitment and effort. This way of thinking prepares the mind for difficulties and promotes learning from mistakes, which encourages creative thinking.

2. Look for a Variety of Experiences

The mind is enriched by a variety of experiences. The mind's horizons are widened by participating in a variety of activities, reading widely, and interacting with diverse people, creating a rich canvas for original thought.

3. Meditation and mindfulness

Using mindfulness and meditation techniques improves cognitive flexibility, lowers stress, and trains the mind to focus. It gets the mind in the right frame of mind for imaginative thinking.

4. Make Use of the Brainstorming Power

A structured method for generating ideas is brainstorming. It can be used as a mental exercise before coming up with ideas to help loosen the mind.

5. Create a Culture of Creativity

Your physical environment has an impact on how you feel. A creative mindset can be fostered in an uncluttered, distraction-free environment.

6. Accept Diverse Points of View

Seeking out different viewpoints should be part of your mental preparation. Interacting with people from various backgrounds and cultures exposes one to new ideas and fresh ways of thinking.

7. Exercises for Creative Thinking

Warming up your mind can be accomplished by participating in creative exercises like word association or ideation games.

8. Ongoing Education and Skill Building

The ability to adapt and be open to new ideas is maintained by continually learning new things. Developing knowledge in a variety of fields gives one a toolbox for original thought.

Mentally Getting Ready for Different Situations

The right kind of mental preparation depends on the situation or challenge at hand. Here, we look at how to mentally get ready for various scenarios:

1. Originality of self

Mental readiness can be used in daily life to improve oneself, pursue interests, and overcome difficulties. Your capacity for coming up with original solutions to everyday issues is improved by mental readiness.

2. Expertise in Creativity

A prepared mind is a valuable asset in the workplace. Planning a project, conducting brainstorming sessions, or addressing challenging issues are all examples of mental preparation. It gives you the tools you need to bring fresh ideas to your group or company.

3. Innovative Issue-Solving

Mental preparation is crucial when solving

problems in creative ways. It makes it possible for you to look at issues differently and come up with fresh solutions.

4. Innovation and the Creative Arts

Creative thinking is essential to writers, innovators, and artists. In order to ensure that inspiration strikes when it is most needed, mental preparation is essential.

Conclusion

The key to unleashing the potential of creativity is to mentally prepare for it. Creativity is a force that can be developed. A ready mind is the secret to thinking creatively in any circumstance, whether you're navigating personal challenges, pursuing professional success, or looking for novel solutions in the larger world. By embracing the many mental preparation techniques, you give yourself the power to approach any situation with the limitless innovation and inspiration that comes from creative thinking.

7. BE CURIOUS AND DEVELOP A PASSION FOR LEARNING

Introduction

Interest is the start that lights imaginative considering. It is the voracious crave to investigate, get it, and learn. Matched with a energy for deep rooted learning, interest gets to be the driving constrain behind development, problem-solving, and individual development. In this article, we dig into the significant significance of being inquisitive and creating a energy for learning in sustaining inventive considering. We'll investigate how these two components, when combined, can open entryways to perpetual conceivable outcomes and upgrade our lives in various ways.

I. The Pith of Interest

1. Interest Unleashed

Interest is the natural human characteristic that drives us to address, to ponder, and to look for answers. It's the constrain that powers our want to investigate the obscure and to form sense of the world around us.

2. The Roots of Imagination

Inventiveness flourishes on interest. It is through the inquiring of questions, the investigation of conceivable outcomes, and the voracious thirst for information that novel thoughts are born. Interest is the portal to imaginative considering.

II. The Part of Deep rooted Learning

1. Deep rooted Learning Characterized

Long lasting learning is the commitment to obtaining information and aptitudes all through one's life. It is the hone of looking for instruction past conventional educate, and it's a vital component in remaining versatile and important in a quickly changing world.

2. Learning as a Deep rooted Travel

Long lasting learning may be a travel, not a goal. It includes the nonstop interest of information, the advancement of unused aptitudes, and the adjustment to advancing circumstances.

III. How Interest and Long lasting Learning Improve Inventive Considering

1. The Cooperative energy of Interest and Learning

When interest and learning come together, they make a energetic collaboration. Interest moves us to explore a endless cluster of subjects and concepts, while lifelong learning prepares us with the devices and information required to create sense of our disclosures.

2. Imaginative Problem-Solving

Interest, coupled with the capacity to memorize, may be a effective combination for problem-solving. When confronted with challenges, inquisitive people who have developed a enthusiasm for learning are more likely to plan imaginative arrangements.

3. Development and Enterprise

Advancement frequently emerges from a persistent interest approximately how things work and a commitment to learning. Entrepreneurs who ceaselessly investigate and extend their information are more likely to form groundbreaking items and administrations.

IV. Developing Interest and Deep rooted Learning

1. Cultivating Interest

Interest can be supported from childhood through a assortment of hones, such as empowering questions, investigating modern encounters, and giving get to to different assets.

2. Creating a Energy for Learning

A enthusiasm for learning can be developed at any age. It includes setting aside time for instruction, looking for out modern challenges, and finding individual inspiration within the interest of information.

V. How Interest and Long lasting Learning Influence Diverse Viewpoints of Life

1. Individual Development and Fulfillment

The combination of interest and deep rooted learning comes about in individual development and fulfillment. It can lead to a more enhanced and important life, as people always find and create modern angles of themselves.

2. Instruction and Career

Inquisitive people who are committed to lifelong learning are way better prepared to exceed expectations in instruction and explore career openings. They adjust more effectively to changes within the work advertise and persistently update their abilities.

Rewrite this text in simpler language. Creativity in the Arts refers to the ability to come up with new and original ideas when it comes to expressing oneself through various forms of art, such as painting, music, dance, and acting. It involves thinking outside of the box and being innovative in order to create something unique and different. Creativity in the Arts allows individuals to explore their imagination and showcase their own personal style and perspective.

Artists and creative people do well when they are curious and always seeking to learn new things. Trying out different ways of doing things, changing how things look and talking about different topics is really important for coming up with new and interesting ideas.

4 Rewrite this passage using simpler language: Scientific and technological advancements refer to the progress made in our understanding of the natural world and the development of new tools and machines.

Invention in science and technology is strongly connected to being curious and gaining knowledge. Scientists and inventors use what previous people have discovered and keep trying to learn more about the world.

VI In plain language: Challenges and obstacles are difficulties or problems that someone may face.

Please simplify my understanding of the text: 1. Overcoming Fear and Apathy means facing our worries and lack of interest.

Some people may feel scared or not care, which stops them from being curious and enthusiastic about learning. To overcome these challenges, you need to change how you think, be okay with feeling uncomfortable, and be dedicated to becoming better.

Please explain what specific text you would like me to rewrite using simpler words. Finding a balance between being curious and staying focused.

Curiosity is strong but sometimes it can cause too much information. Finding a balance between being curious and studying with a purpose is really important for learning things effectively.

7th The effect of wanting to learn and constantly learning throughout life on society

1. Rewrite this text using easier words: A society that is more creative and inventive.

When people in a group are interested in learning new things throughout their lives, it encourages a culture where new ideas and inventions can thrive. This can help us make progress in many different areas, like technology, science, art, and society.

Rewrite this text using simpler words: 2. Getting better at solving problems and making decisions.

A community that values and encourages curiosity and learning is more capable of finding solutions to difficult problems and making wise choices. This helps you think carefully and be able to adjust when things change.

Eight The digital age refers to the current time period where technology and digital tools are widely used. In this age, there are many chances to learn new things.

Please simplify the following text: 1. The results of the study indicated a significant correlation between the variables, suggesting a strong connection between them. Technology has improved a lot and we now have more ways to get information.

The digital age has made it easier than ever to get information and learn new things. The way we learn has been greatly changed by the internet, e-learning platforms, and digital libraries.

2 Rewrite this passage using simpler language: Problems in the Digital Era

The digital age gives us many chances to learn, but it also brings problems, like having too much information to process and the need to understand how to use digital tools. It is important to know how to use online resources well.

Summary

Being curious and wanting to learn throughout your life are key to being able to think creatively. When you put them together, they can change people, communities, and the whole world. By being curious, always wanting to learn more, and making a commitment to keep learning throughout our lives, we can bring out our ability to come up with new ideas, grow personally, and make progress in society. The strong desire for learning and the openness to explore new things are what motivate us to think creatively and make a better future.

8- TRUSTING YOUR MIND AND NOT WAITING FOR INSPIRATION

A Brief Introduction

Imaginative considering is frequently depicted as an tricky drive that strikes like a lightning jolt, taking off us holding up for motivation to light our minds. In any case, in reality, imagination may be an expertise that can be developed, harnessed, and coordinated by trusting your intellect, instead of depending exclusively on scattered bursts of motivation. In this broad investigation, we dig into the significant significance of trusting your intellect and not holding up for motivation as the establishment of imaginative considering. We'll unwind how this approach engages people to tap into their intrinsic imaginative potential, cultivating advancement, problem-solving, and individual development in different features of life.

I. The Myths of Imaginative Motivation

1. The Myth of the "Eureka" Minute

The notion that inventive thoughts strike all of a sudden and without caution could be a common misguided judgment. In truth, inventive considerations regularly advance through a more think and supported cognitive handle.

2. The Holding up Amusement

Numerous people hold the conviction that they must hold up for motivation to begin their inventive endeavors. This inactive approach can smother inventive potential and lead to dissatisfaction.

II. The Inventive Intellect: A Wellspring of Advancement

1. Trusting Your Intellect

Trusting your intellect as a fertile ground for inventiveness is the establishment of this approach. It includes grasping your cognitive capacities and realizing merely possess the capacity to produce imaginative thoughts.

2. The Control of Instinct

Instinct, regularly seen as a strange component of the imaginative handle, could be a item of the intuitive intellect. Trusting your instinct can lead to significant bits of knowledge and novel arrangements.

III. Overcoming Creative Blocks

1. The Clear Canvas Disorder

Imaginative pieces are common, and numerous individuals involvement them. Trusting your intellect can assist you explore through these challenging periods by centering on the method instead of fixating over a idealize result.

2. Grasping Blemish

The fear of flaw can ruin inventive considering. Learning to grasp and indeed celebrate imperfection can free your inventive intellect.

IV. The Part of Mentality in Imaginative Considering

1. Development Attitude

A development attitude, the conviction that capacities can be created through devotion and difficult work, is vital for trusting your mind. It empowers strength within the confront of inventive challenges.

2. Developing a Positive Attitude

A positive attitude cultivates a sustaining

environment for imaginative considering. It permits people to approach inventive endeavors with eagerness and openness.

V. Trusting Your Intellect totally Different Perspectives of Life

1. Individual Development

Trusting your mind is an indispensably portion of personal development. It permits people to investigate their claim potential, go up against challenges, and adjust to advancing circumstances.

2. Instruction and Career

Within the field of instruction and proficient improvement, the capacity to believe your intellect can lead to superior learning results, career movement, and inventive commitments within the working environment.

3. Imagination within the Expressions

The expressions flourish on the concept of trusting your intellect. Craftsmen and makers frequently depend on their inside assets to precise themselves and bring their thoughts to life.

4. Logical and Mechanical Headways

Within the world of science and innovation, advancement stems from the believe put in one's cognitive capacities. Researchers and creators who believe their minds are more likely to form groundbreaking disclosures.

VI. The Inventive Prepare: A Guided Travel

1. Setting Objectives and Eagerly

Building up clear objectives and eagerly gives a guide for inventive considering. It gives course to your endeavors and minimizes diversions.

2. Engagement and Perseverance

Effectively locks in with a imaginative challenge and enduring in your endeavors are significant angles of this approach. Trusting your intellect implies remaining committed to the method indeed when comes about appear tricky.

VII. The Affect of Trusting Your Intellect on Society

1. A Culture of Development

People who believe their minds and

empower this approach in others contribute to a culture of advancement. This cultivates societal progressions and problem-solving.

2. Engaging the Another Era

Encouraging younger eras to believe their minds can have a significant affect on long haul. It prepares them with the skills and attitude required for inventive considering.

VIII. Supporting Your Imaginative Intellect within the Computerized Age

1. Innovation as a Instrument for Imaginative Considering

Within the computerized age, innovation can serve as a capable instrument for upgrading imaginative considering. It gives get to to a riches of data and collaboration openings.

2. Advanced Diversions

Whereas innovation offers benefits, it also introduces distractions that can hinder the trust you put in your intellect. Overseeing computerized diversions is key to cultivating inventive considering.

IX. Challenges in Trusting Your Intellect

1. Self-Doubt

Overcoming self-doubt could be a challenge confronted by numerous within the prepare of trusting their minds. Methodologies to boost self-confidence are essential.

2. Fear of Disappointment

The fear of disappointment can be paralyzing. Recognizing that disappointment is portion of the inventive prepare and learning from it is fundamental to trusting your intellect.

Conclusion

Trusting your intellect and not holding up for motivation could be a capable approach to imaginative considering. It may be a proactive mentality that recognizes the boundless potential inside each person. By grasping this approach, people can tap into their inventive supplies, cultivate development, overcome deterrents, and involvement individual development. In doing so, they contribute to a culture of advancement and societal advance.

Trusting your intellect isn't only a procedure; it's a worldview move that enables people to tackle their intrinsic inventiveness and shape a brighter future.

9. LEARN TO IGNORE PROBLEMS

Introduction

Imaginative considering is regularly related with problem-solving. In any case, there's a catch 22 at play: now and then, the key to opening imagination lies in learning to disregard issues. This article dives into the significant significance of specifically tuning out issues to sustain imaginative considering. We'll investigate how this irrational approach can open entryways to advancement, novel points of view, and individual development.

I. The Myth of Never-ending Problem-Solving

1. The Faction of Problem-Solving

Society places a tall premium on problem-solving. We are conditioned to accept that tending to issues head-on is the essential way to victory.

2. The Weight of Consistent Arrangements

The tireless center on tackling issues can lead to uneasiness, burnout, and a smothering of imagination. The weight to continuously have answers hampers imaginative considering.

II. Grasping Cognitive Opportunity

1. Selective Ignorance

Learning to disregard issues, at slightest incidentally, is around giving your intellect the opportunity to meander. It is the consider choice to redirect your consideration from prompt challenges.

2. Cognitive Space

By making cognitive space, you permit your intellect to wind, make associations, and investigate thoughts. This mental delay can lead to unforeseen experiences.

III. Disparate Considering and Inventiveness

1. Disparate Considering Characterized

Disparate considering is the capacity to produce a wide cluster of thoughts by investigating numerous arrangements and viewpoints.

2. The Part of Divergent Thinking in Inventiveness

Unique considering could be a inventive catalyst. By evading issues, you energize your intellect to meander openly, cultivating inventiveness.

IV. Getting away Mental Traps

1. Mental Grooves

Always tending to issues can lead to mental trenches, where your thinking gets to be kept and monotonous.

2. The Control of Point of view Move

Learning to disregard issues energizes you to move your point of view and elude these mental grooves. This move can open unused approaches and new thoughts.

V. Creativity and the Control of Play

1. Play as a Inventive Outlet

Play, or unstructured investigation, could be a pivotal portion of the inventive prepare. Disregarding issues can make space for play.

2. Breakthroughs in Play

Chronicled cases of inventive breakthroughs that developed from perky investigation emphasize the control of overlooking issues to cultivate inventiveness.

VI. Adjusting Numbness and Obligation

1. The Duty of Tending to Issues

Overlooking issues doesn't cruel dodging duties or avoiding imperative issues. It's almost finding a adjust between tending to challenges and supporting inventiveness.

2. The Freedom of Prioritization

Prioritization permits for a more purposefulness center on the issues that require quick consideration, freeing inventive vitality for other ranges.

VII. Application in Individual Development

1. Development Past Problem-Solving

Individual development expands past tending to issues. Disregarding certain issues can make openings for self-discovery and improvement.

2. Mindfulness and Self-Reflection

Mindfulness hones, self-reflection, and contemplation are devices that can help in learning to disregard issues when required.

VIII. Cultivating a Culture of Inventiveness

1. Empowering Inventive Investigation

Organizations and communities can advanceimagination by empowering people to investigate past the limits of issues.

2. The Part of Authority

Pioneers who esteem inventive considering must create an environment where group individuals feel secure to investigate thoughts and every so often overlook issues.

IX. Challenges in Grasping Numbness

1. Fear of Results

A critical challenge in learning to disregard issues is the fear of potential results. It can be overwhelming to intentionally occupy consideration from issues that request determination.

2. Overcoming the Fear

Overcoming the fear of results includes building a versatile attitude, understanding the potential benefits, and cultivating a culture that acknowledges transitory numbness.

X. The Computerized Age and Data Over-burden

1. Data Over-burden

The advanced age has exacerbated the weight to always unravel issues. Data over-burden can overpower imaginative thinking.

2. Computerized Detox and Mental Space

Hones like advanced detox and data sifting can make mental space for overlooking issues when essential.

XI. Victory Stories in Inventive Obliviousness

1. Chronicled Cases

Verifiable illustrations from different areas, such as science, craftsmanship, and trade, highlight how disregarding issues driven to groundbreaking accomplishments.

2. Advanced Occasions

Advanced occasions of imaginative scholars who specifically overlooked issues to fortify imaginative considering are inspected.

<u>Conclusion</u>

The art of learning to disregard issues is an unusual way to cultivating imagination. It's about giving your intellect the flexibility to wander, permitting it to investigate strange domain and make modern associations. By grasping this approach, you not as it were diminish the weight to always illuminate issues but moreover free your imaginative potential. The capacity to specifically overlook issues can lead to development, novel points of view, and personal development. It's a confusing travel that engages people to think exterior the box and shape a brighter future.